Maximizing and Taking Control of Your Path

GET OFF THE COUCH

DR. MARITSA YZAGUIRRE-KELLEY

Get Off the Couch

Dr. Maritsa Yzaguirre-Kelley

Get Off the Couch

Copyright © 2017 by Maritsa Yzaguirre-Kelley

This book is not intended as a substitute for the medical advice of physicians. The reader should regularly consult a physician in matters relating to his/her health and particularly with respect to any symptoms which may require diagnosis or medical attention.

Printed in the United States of America
First Printing, 2017

Credit for the photographer
Crystal Swass at Blue Anchor Photography
www.Blueanchorlove.com
Crystal@blueanchorlove.com
Edit & Formatting by: LC Taylor Publishings @
www.lctaylorpublishings.com

Dedication

I would like to thank my wonderful and loving family for supporting me in my journey to success. Without them, it would be impossible for me to do what I do and help others get off the couch.

Table of Contents

Dedication ____iii

Introduction ____1

Chapter 1: Why Seek Therapy?____3

    What Causes People to Finally Seek Help? ______________________________3
    What's the best way to work subconscious or conscious mind? _________7

Chapter 2: How to Choose the Right Therapist ________________________________11

    How do People Find a Therapist?_______________________________________11
    How Can People Choose the Right Therapist?__________________________13
    What Are Unethical Practices in Terms of Therapy? ___________________19
    What you don't want to happen:_______________________________________19

Chapter 3: What Do People Want to Do in Therapy? ___________________________23

    What Drives People to Finally Seek Help? ______________________________23
    Do People Know What They Want to Do? ______________________________25
    How Can Education Change Things? ___________________________________27

Chapter 4: What is the difference between coaching and therapy? _________31

    What is the Proper Behavior for Interacting with a Coach or Therapist? __33
    Why do Many Clients Fail at Coaching and also at Therapy? ___________33
    What is the Missing Ingredient in the Sauce for Real and Meaningful
    Change? ____34

Chapter 5: Breakthrough Techniques____36

    The History of Psychology ____36
    The History of Hypnotism____37
    What is NLP?____40
    Richard Bandler: The Father of NLP ___________________________________41
    What is So Different About NLP? ______________________________________42
    The Subjectivity of the World____42
    How Are These Techniques Used for Real Change? ___________________44
    Change According to the Doctor ______________________________________44
    The Work of Dr. Maritsa Yzaguirre-Kelley ____________________________45

Chapter 6: How to Get Your Clients off The Couch ___________________________47

What Will Facilitate Permanent Change? _______________________________ 47

Using NLP and Hypnotism for Real Change _____________________________ 52

The Magic of the Mind with Darren Brown _____________________________ 54

New Discoveries About Harry Houdini__________________________________ 55

Afterthought NLP Unlocking the Value _________________________________ 57

The Power of NLP and Hypnosis____ 58

Chapter 7: Services of Dr. Yzaguirre-Kelley ___________________________ **59**

Alternative Therapies and Retreats ___________________________________ 59

Counselling Solutions ____ 59

Health and Holistic Practices ____ 60

The Impact of Nutrition on Your Health________________________________ 61

Substance Abuse and Health Issues ___________________________________ 61

About the Author ____ **62**

Introduction

By the time people seek therapy, they're often at a point of pain. Many have tried everything from self-medication to alternative methods, which weren't overseen by a professional. All the individual knows is pain, whether physical or emotional. Many factors keep people from seeking assistance, some of them are financial, personal pride, and others are them refusing to acknowledge a problem.

When the individual finally makes it onto the 'couch' of the therapist, there are many questions, and not many solutions. It becomes critical for the client to have confidence in the professional working with them, as well as, having faith in the methods and practice that us used. 'If you lean the ladder on the wrong wall, every step you make will continue to be in the wrong direction'.

Many clients find themselves on the professional's couch, unsure of how they got there. Often, they don't understand what steps need to come next. Instead of outlining the path to their solution, many clients do not know what to ask or what to expect. They spend years coming back and discussing the same issues, without any forward movement or eliciting real change.

I'm not recreating some revolutionary method. What I've done is to incorporate proven methods to my sessions. These methods work with getting clients to where they want to be, without wasting a lot of time and money. This changes everything about the way therapy is applied as well as the way the client is treated.

Get Off the Couch

The techniques I utilize are based on the use of the subconscious mind, mind body techniques, a blending of hypnosis, NLP, and other techniques, which can change your life in virtually no time.

There is no for years in therapy, stewing over every issue you've ever experienced in life. In fact, those behaviors can be traumatizing if relived over and over. Working with the wrong person a can make it worst NOT better.

If you are ready to 'get off the couch', as well as ensuring you're going to affect real change, you're reading the right book. If you're tired of putting a bandage on a bullet wound, and you're ready for real transformation, keep reading. This book will help promote change and lead you to the happy life you deserve. I'm happy to help you through the process to affect real change in your life.

Let's get started!

Before we begin, **Click here** to sign up for my **Newsletter** and receive news and updates which will help you stay on the path to happiness!

Chapter 1: Why Seek Therapy?

The ideal reason people seek therapy, would be to get to know themselves. This age-old quest, of finding oneself, is what prompted some of the greatest poems. It also led many wandering heroes of classical times, to seek out oracles across foreign lands. This is not a love story, nor is it an epic poem, it's REAL life.

Although the worlds of philosophy still have their place, inscribed in the walls of the temple at Delphi for example, who has time when they are trying to pay bills, raise children, and live a real life? Who is searching for self-improvement in a way that allows them to seek out the books and the couches of one therapist to the other?

Everyone has things about themselves they hate. Or things which drive them crazy, yet at the end of the day there is a big difference between having an annoyance with an issue, and having something affect your daily life. But when do you know you need to seek therapy?

What Causes People to Finally Seek Help?

When it comes to making sure you're, happy and fulfilled in life, most people struggle with identifying what they need. It's very clear everyone has periods of stress, sadness, and difficulties identifying when there's a problem. Many people seek help, but many never will. One in five Americans need therapy, but will never seek any. Of the Americans who need therapy, currently 45% are in counseling. There are barriers to people getting counseling. The fact is most people could benefit from talking to therapist. So why is therapy thought of as a luxury not a necessity?

It's important to make sure if you're feeling in immediate danger of hurting yourself or others, you call 911 or go to your closest hospital. Things usually will get worse for the client if they are avoiding and they are not seeking counseling on a regular basis. What that also means is it's important to get counseling for the individuals as soon as possible.

Many people are afraid to get counseling. Due to the many myths surrounding the idea of counseling as well as to the idea of seeking help, most avoid seeking out help. The thought of seeking counseling, or if they're going to get help, they'll be branded as "crazy" or as being weak.

Some clients believe therapy won't be helpful for them, or they may think real results are impossible in the long run. All the fears associated with counseling can become a reality, if individuals aren't careful about who they seek out for a therapist.

Counseling, depending on the condition or situation, can be expensive. It may not be covered by their health plan. More therapists are choosing not to be 'in network'. This is due to low reimbursement rates and the hassle of dealing with insurance companies. Most therapist, however, are willing to work with clients by negotiate rates on a sliding fee scale - especially if the client is committed to the process. There are many community mental health centers available, but use caution when using these as the staff tend to be over worked, underpaid, and the turnover rate is usually high.

Get Off the Couch

A key point that's important to remember is, people often fail to link mental health equally important as exercising and diet. The benefits of therapy are like other stress relievers and need to be seen in that way. It's important for the client to recognize when it's time to set up an appointment and get help.

Here are some of the key signs it's time to seek professional help.

❖ Everything Happening to You Feels Overly Intense.

If you feel overwhelmed, or you are becoming overwhelmed by your feelings, you may find you have other issues at hand. When it comes to intensity, there are often signs or symptoms you should watch for. One of the signs is displaced energy called catastrophizing. This is a form of displaced energy, meaning you are seeing everything in the worst possible way – simply put, you blow everything out of proportion.

When a client experiences catastrophizing, they will not be able to function, often leading to long-term issues. This lends to the importance of seeking therapy.

❖ You've Suffered a Trauma

Trauma is a very subjective topic. It can occur a real-life event or from a perceived event. If you've suffered trauma, whether caused by a death, a rape, or any other devastating event, it's important to make sure you process and reframe the incident. Reframing means you will ensure you engage and get help, and avoid pulling away from those around you. You want to make sure you can sit down, and to unpack the events in a way you will be able to have more engagement. If you find yourself not sleeping or avoiding others, it's time to get help.

❖ Issues with Your Immune System

Your body can be affected by when you are emotionally upset. Often physical symptoms of depression can show up as a part of your daily life. Many times, we hold the stress in our bodies, as the body is the unconscious mind. You need to make sure you are taking the time to stop and recognize the various kinds of stress. Remember, stress appears not only in the physical sense, but also in the emotional sense.

❖ Your Abusing or Becoming Dependent

Whether you realize it or not, taking in larger quantities of drugs or alcohol, engaging in reckless sexual behavior, gambling, overeating, or many other forms of self-harm, you are engaging in self-abuse. It is imperative you seek help. These behaviors are not just dangerous for you, but they are a danger to those around you.

❖ You Have Negative Feedback from Your Employer

If you are dealing with problems related to your performance at work, it could be directly linked to your emotional state. You may not be able to pay attention in the way you were before when you are struggling with stress. Getting back on track, by seeking help, will ensure your job performance is where it should be.

❖ You Feel Disconnected from Others

If you feel like you don't want to be a part of activities, that once meant something to you, you may be suffering from stress. You want to make sure you are going to have access to the best assistance.

❖ If Your Relationships Are in Trouble

Communication is key to a healthy relationship. Understanding your feelings in the moment, are essential to speaking your feelings clearly to your partner. If your interactions leave you feeling hopeless, a non-bias third party may need to help you work through the issue. A third party can help you phrase and word things in a non-threatening manner, often eliminating problems.

❖ Your Friends Tell You They Are Worried

Are your friends telling you they're worried? This is a key indicator you may need some help. When your friends are talking, you need to be listening. They are seeing things from the outside and may be recognizing you need help before you realize you do. Listen to them. They are trying to help.

What's the best way to work subconscious or conscious mind?

When it comes to finding the best way to work, one thing to be considered is the how to get the best long-term results with your counselor. Many different counselors choose to work with different techniques, which means the end results for them are going to be the same. It's best to look at the basics. What is the conscious mind? What is the subconscious mind? And why is one preferable to the other?

Get Off the Couch

❖ What is the Conscious Mind?

In traditional psychology, Freud believed the conscious mind was everything that encompassed the awareness of the individual. That meant looking at all the feelings, as well as the sensations accompanying the experiences of the world, and everything around an individual.

When it comes to the mind, there are things the conscious mind works hard to prevent the subconscious mind from seeing. This means there are many emotions and thoughts disguised in the form of dreams, that leak their way across barriers over time. The waking mind guides us, which is the basis for many models of psychology most doctors practice these days.

When looking at the mind, there are many secrets which must be unlocked. There are many things discovered through the process of therapy, and becomes a step by step process of looking at the conscious mind and everything associated.

Much like peeling the layers of an onion, a lot of work is needed when you're using traditional psychology. Much of the behavioral psychology is based on changing the top layers of the mind, but never looks at reprogramming the most basic layers of the brain.

❖ What is the Subconscious Mind?

When you are looking at the mind, the layer everyone knows as personality, actions, and ego is the conscious mind. The layer underneath, however, is the layer responsible for the fundamental programming of information. It is the layer which makes up who a person is at the most basic level.

Get Off the Couch

There are many techniques which can be used to ensure the most basic levels of the brain are being tapped into. When communicating with the subconscious mind, it becomes possible to speak to the person at the most fundamental level.

The process of speaking to the subconscious mind is known as hypnotherapy. This allows direct communication between the therapist and the client.

That direct line of communication opens the door for new way of communication, ensuring the client possibilities of a quick change or instant results.

When it comes to looking at traditional psychology versus hypnotherapy, hypnotherapy is faster. This is because its dealing with the process of the mind in a way other methods of communication are not able to match. It provides alternate ways to access the mind, in a way other methods can't. Hypnotherapy provides a variety of results, where other methods might have failed with the same client

❖ What is Direct Communication in Hypnotherapy?

It becomes challenging to ensure a clear conversation with the subconscious mind. There are many ways in which this is possible, both fast and effective methods to talk to the brain directly. These methods can be accelerated by using medicine, or incorporating other methods.

There are varying opinions about how the human psyche functions. These opinions spark debates about how the various methods work. It's important to note, there are many hypnotherapists who can make sure they go beyond the programming and avoid the excuses made by a client. There are countless variables which can lend to the success of hypnotism.

 "Every person's map of the word is as unique as their thumb print. There are no two people alike. No two people who understand the same sentence the same way…So in dealing with people, you try not to fit them to your concept of what they should be." Milton H. Erickson

Chapter 2: How to Choose the Right Therapist

When it comes to choosing the right therapist, many people miss the purpose from the beginning. Simply put, they do not do their homework. Clients need to find out what the specialty of the therapist is, and in addition, they need to consider how important this decision is. When you consider you're giving someone unfettered access to your mind, and to the way you operate, you are asking that person to help you find a cure for the situation that is ailing you – take this matter seriously!

From the beginning, you should seek someone who is going to be a revolutionary, and someone who is going to be in your corner through the entire process. You cannot simply choose a therapist in the way you would choose a pair of shoes or a handbag. You need to understand the greater reason behind why you are there, who you are picking, and what role the therapist is going to play in your life before you decide on who you want to use.

How do People Find a Therapist?

By the time most people are searching for a therapist, it's clear situations have gotten out of hand. One of the biggest mistakes people make, is they are ready to jump right in and will go and see anyone in their insurance directory. Just because someone is in your directory does not mean they are the right choice for you. Think about it – would you let a veterinarian do major surgery on you just because they went to medical school? NO, so don't pick a therapist lightly.

❖ Why Just Not Go with The Insurance Company
   Suggestion?

Sit down for just a moment to pause and think about how it
sounds. You have no knowledge of this therapist, other than
they work in counseling. Would you simply walk into and office
and hope someone could assist you with something so
personal like therapy? Chances are you wouldn't. You would
also never give such little regard to your mind and to the way it
works.

When a therapist gets calls from new clients, it's important to
make sure the therapist is taking into consideration just
because a new client is taken, it doesn't mean it is going to be
a good fit. It is in some ways the responsibility of the client, as
well as the therapist, to make sure it's the best fit for the client
in the long run.

When the client is willing to hold a discussion with the
therapist about the pros and the cons of getting counseling,
there are many people willing to make sure they are in good
hands. Unfortunately, most are not willing to take a chance on
a therapist they cannot use their insurance with. This often
changes when clients find other providers are booked for
months in advance, or is something too difficult for them to be
able to handle.

It is important to make sure when medical attention is needed,
the individual who needs the attention can get it. A large part
of this is that by the time someone has made the decision to
seek help, they are already in a place of needing assistance in
a short time frame.

Get Off the Couch

❖ You Must Have a Diagnosis of a Mental Issue

Many insurance companies will only provide services in a situation when the service is medically necessary. Essentially, if you are going to use your insurance, you must first prove you are not able to function daily. This means you need to show your mental health is affecting the quality of your life.

There are many reasons you may be having difficulty with life. You need to know what you are doing is what is best for you, and you need to ensure you will be able to show why it's going to be difficult for you. You will not be able to use excuses like, 'I am not doing well'. Instead, you need to make sure you are getting counseling for something specifically affecting you and allow you to be happy with the results.

Many people may be thinking why not just be diagnosed with the condition, but that is very unethical. Many people who will just give the diagnosis are not people you want to be surrounded by. This means you need to make sure you are seeing an ethical doctor, not just anyone who is on the list of your insurance at the time.

How Can People Choose the Right Therapist?

When you are looking for the right therapist takes time and effort. You want to make sure you can find the right person for you, specifically someone you are going click with. Think about it…. you are asking someone to do important work in your mind and you are trusting them not to screw up. You want to ensure you are getting the best person to help you and you want to know who you are working with.

Get Off the Couch

Just looking through the insurance directory is the worst
possible way to go about things. It's very important to make
sure you follow basic guidelines to produce the best results.
Here are a few pointers to help you to be able to find the best
therapist who will likely mesh with your needs, your
personality, as well as your future:

✓ Talk to Your Family and Friends

If other family and friends aver sought therapy, talk to them
about what it was they loved or hated about their experience.
Many of the best referrals for doctors are going from other
clients. If you have talked to people and you are not getting
any good responses, make sure you are looking at the
persona and seeing how controversial they are in the various
stages of therapy.

You want to make sure you have called local establishments
available to you. There are many establishments which
specialize in diverse lines of counseling, which means you can
find the right choice, for the right therapist and method.

You want to make sure you are not just getting someone who
is going to be convenient. You want to make sure you are
finding someone who is the right fit for you. If you must make
a long drive to see the right person, do it. It will be worth it
versus seeing someone who is close to you, but not the fit you
need.

✓ Do Your Homework Online

You want to make sure you take the time and you find the
right therapist. Take your time to read up on all the therapists

in your area and see what you can do to find the best fit for you.

✓ Look at Therapist Finder

When you are looking online you want to make sure you are looking at the photos of the therapist to seeing if you can connect with them. You do not want to work with a therapist who looks as though they are posing as a model; instead, you want to work with someone who offers a real look at who they are and what they do. You want to be able to look at your therapist and feel comfortable with them – listen to your gut.

✓ Consider the Gender of Your Therapist

When you are speaking with someone about some of the most intimate areas of your life, it is important to make sure you are comfortable with the material you are discussing.

You may need to have a discussion, given a certain situation involving a certain gender. You want to make sure you can work with the therapist without their gender affecting the result. You want to make be open and honest, as well as completely unfiltered with your therapist, which means gender is essential in your consideration of who to see.

✓ Area of Study and Theory

It is hard to plan when there is such a wide variety in specialties related to therapy. You need to make sure you know what kind of assistance you need, and what kind of area of practice is going to be the most effective for your desired outcome. Here are a few guidelines to help you select the right type of therapist:

If you are looking at issues with behavior, it's important to determine if you are looking at whether it is unconscious or not. If it is, you may need a psychodynamic therapist can use methods such as hypnotism.

A Cognitive Therapist would be someone to help you unravel your tangled thoughts. These are therapists who look at the way that you think and help you reprogram your actions. When you chose not to talk to family members or friends you trust, you may want to work with someone who deals with family or conflict resolution.

There are many classifications of therapists out there. It is imperative to seek out family and friends input, as well as getting referrals from others to ensure you have access to the best choice. Make sure you find the right person and the right style of therapy to facilitate growth with you.

- ✓ Call the Therapist

Once you find a therapist you like, you want to make sure you call them and speak to them about their practice and their methods. Here is what you need to make sure you are aware of when calling:

Once you decide, have their number on hand so you can make a call.

Find out where he or she went to school. You will see the best schools do not always mean the best fit; however, you want to make sure the person went to an accredited school before becoming part of their practice.

Make sure you know the specialty of the therapist. There are many therapists who spread themselves too broadly, which means you will not find who will meet all your needs.

Know if the therapist has worked with people who have the same issues as you. Make sure when you are on the phone, you share a little about what it is you are planning to discuss or needing from them.

Know what the therapist has received training for. Also find out what kind of seminars and other events the therapist has attended. You want to ensure] you are getting the right fit. If you are with someone who does not have enough experience, you need to hang up the phone and move on to the next person.

Make sure the therapist you are working with is licensed or certified. The reason for this is, there are many counselors who are not licensed or certified and are practicing. This is something may surprise you, but you want to ensure you are checking on the credentials of the person you are selecting.

❖ Has your therapist gone into therapy?

If you are seeing a therapist, you should expect that he or she has done their own work and has had therapy. Otherwise you will find there are many issues, as well as, many other issues will arise with time.

When you are considering setting up an appointment, you want to discuss the fees and any sliding scales available, especially if you are having a hard time paying the premium. Talk with the therapist about the rate, and in the event, you are not able to afford them, speak to the therapist about a more affordable rate.

You will find there are many therapists who will to refer you to others who may be more affordable. Again, even when getting a referral to a more cost-effective therapist, you want to make sure they fit your check list.

✓ Follow your Intuition

You want to make sure you are following your intuition and that you know you are making the right choice. If you are feeling nervous or strange when you are on the phone with the therapist, this may not be the right choice for you. You will find you may feel a little odd at first, which is normal. However, if it does not feel like a good fit you may not want to make an appointment.

When you sit down with the therapist you want to make sure you can talk to them and you feel they are listening to you. You want to make sure you are at peace with them as well, and you know you can talk in an open and unguarded way.

You need to make sure you are going to find the perfect fit for you to really make progress.

What Are Unethical Practices in Terms of Therapy?

Much like the unethical practices in business, there are also unethical practices in therapy. It is important to know how to spot an unethical therapist from the beginning. Here are things you need to look out for, to make sure you are not falling prey to one of these 'therapists'.

It is always easier to see those who are doing a good job, than it is to see those who are doing a bad job. There are many kinds of behavior which are unprofessional. That means as a client, you want to safeguard by looking out for these behaviors to guarantee you make real progress.

There are many things that you make an ethical therapist when you are working with a professional. A few of these indicators include a smile, a handshake, and the complete attention of the therapist.

What you don't want to happen:

✓ Your Therapist Ignores Your Needs.

Many times, it is very easy to ensure that you are ignoring the situation as well as ignoring the way that you are being treated. It may be the therapist is cheap, or there is a rate that you are enjoying. Whatever the case may be, it's important to realize that you cannot turn your back on bad behavior.

✓ Don't Make Excuses for Them!

As the client, it is important to ensure you are not making excuses for dysfunctional relationships that you find yourself a part of. If the behavior is consistent, it is not a good fit – end of story.

Whether you know it or not, when you are making excuses for the therapist, you are committing cognitive dissonance. This happens when you are holding two different ideas about something.

You want to make sure that you can have access to the best relationship with your therapist. You need to make sure that you don't have any negative feelings about him or her. You are working with someone who is doing deep work and you need to make sure that you are being picky.

You want to make sure if you are in the role of a caregiver, that you are super careful about the professional who is going to be doing work with your loved one. Make sure you are working with the right professional and doing your homework well in advance.

✓ Talking on Their Cell Phone While You Are in Session:

Your therapist should give you their undivided attention. It is not possible for you to make progress if your therapist is detached from your sessions. You need to have another doctor if this is occurring. If there is an emergency that happens, you want to make sure you can move on to the next topic in the conversation as soon as possible.

✓ They Are Self Consumed!

If you are speaking with a therapist who keeps imposing his or her stories on top of yours, you may need a new therapist. The main reason for the therapists may try to be seeking common ground, but instead they may just come across as egotistical. Stories can be used for learning, but the session should not be consumed with the therapist talking about themselves.

Get Off the Couch

✓   Not Returning Your Calls in a Reasonable Time!

Make sure that you are observing the time being dedicated to you and that you know you are a priority. In the event you are reaching out to your therapist, and you are not getting any feedback, you will see you need to move on. You may have a moment when you really need the assistance of a therapist and you may not have access to one.

✓   Crossing Lines!

One thing important to consider is many professionals out there are slightly unprofessional and may be crossing a line with flirting or some other similar situation.

Make sure you are working with a professional therapist and not one who is going to present themselves in any context that is not 100% professional.

✓   Keeping the Client in the Chair

When it comes to the most unethical practices, one of them is keeping the client in the chair when they no longer need therapy. Instead of working for the progress of the client, many therapists simply never learned how to run their businesses. For that reason, they are willing to keep a client in the chair after they have made progress to the point they are ready to leave. A therapist needs to take the time to look hard at their business, as well as ensure they have planned an exit strategy for every client as they come into the door.

"I do not think that there is any other quality so essential to success of any kind as the quality of perseverance. It overcomes almost everything, even nature." - John D. Rockefeller

Chapter 3: What Do People Want to Do in Therapy?

When it comes to seeking therapy, the individual knows he or she needs change. What may not be immediately clear to him or her, is what kind of change is necessary. Many things happen to a person daily that will let them know a change is needed. It might be personal relationships are suffering or it might be issues with a job.

All people know is that there is something going on and they need to find a solution in for the problem. There are many people, before coming to therapy, believe they have tried 'everything'. Maybe they've tried acupuncture, meditation, or other methods to no avail. They may not understand what the issue is, therefore not understand how to fix the problem. When someone finally comes into therapy, they are looking for a solution that will end their pain or problem.

Many of the other tools and other methods have been exhausted, lending to way which ensures there is a new set of solutions for the issue at hand.

What Drives People to Finally Seek Help?

Whether or not we want to admit it, the greatest driver of change is pain. When something is not working, it often manifests itself in a way which means real change is required for the person, and there must be instant.

Get Off the Couch

That's the time the client seeks a solution and does not know what to do. All the client knows in that moment, is that something hurts and there must be a way to change it. There is not always an immediate answer to what causes people to seek help – other than pain.

Sometimes it manifests from difficult situations in their lives; other times it comes from the way that something may emerge from the memory of a situation that may have caused a need to reframe the position or the experience in the mind of the person.

There are many reasons people have pain and there are many benefits that come from the pain. There has been a lot of research from studies about the way people are able to react to situations with awareness. When there is an awareness of how a situation affects a person, there is also a way to ensure it is possible for there to be cooperation in how to respond to it.

People are ready to respond to their environments and the situations that are based around their surroundings. In one example, there was a comparison of looking at the way people were responding in competition versus in cooperation. In situations where the term cooperation was used, there was a completely different response to having others around.

There are some situations in which people respond in ways they do not understand, and which means it is important to find out why there are those kinds of responses on a regular basis. There are reasons that people will some sometimes act competitively, and other times will cooperate.

Get Off the Couch

At the end of the day it is based on the behavior of the individual and it is important to see that some of this has nothing to do with improper behavior and instead has everything to do with the way that behavior is being processed. Sometimes it is also very clear that the way that we may respond to a situation may be because we are feeling sad or anxious and that it is important to get to the root of it. Some people have developed unhealthy behaviors to life situations. If we can change those reactions, we can change the consequences.

When it comes to seeking therapy, it is all about understanding the why in that situation and getting to the bottom of knowing how that the behavior can then be codified into a plan to ensure that there is a disentanglement from actions that are painful and a way that you will then be able to move forward with treating others in the way that you should.

Do People Know What They Want to Do?

According to Forbes, only 3% of people out there know what they want out of life. This is because around only 3% of people plan and execute on goals in the long term to ensure that they are going to be able to achieve what they are shooting for in their personal and in their professional lives. What this staggering figure amounts to, is many people who have no idea what they want and what they need in their lives to ensure that they are satisfied or that they have a way to move forward in happiness.

This does not just mean that people are not getting what they want from their jobs but also that they are not getting what they want in their relationships. When one part of a life begins to suffer, even if it is from lack of planning, the other areas also begin to have issues. The oracle at Delphi had one lasting piece of advice for weary travelers that came searching for advice… 'Know Thyself'.

These are words that have echoed down the corridors of history from 5th century BCE to current day, to get man to take a moment and pause and figure out the goals of life since it can pass in the blink of an eye. This means from early life there was always a lot of planning for the Greeks.

One thing that happens today is the cookie cutter sort of existence for all who are going to be a part of the professional world. It is expected that a person will go to college, get a job, have children, and become a productive member of society.

Unlike the great quests of literature and unlike the great epics of the past, western society is often devoid of those milestones that helped to plan the journey in the past. As many native cultures have traditions like walkabouts.

It is a time when a young person can go off into the wilderness and then to decide what it is that he or she is wanting to do with their life. There are many plans and many adventures that are held in these times that have become case along the wayside in modern culture.

It is hard to imagine that most children know themselves when they go off to college. Since research has shown that the brain is not completely formed and does not understand the complete value or consequences of risk until the age of 25 it is easy to see why there is so much question as to desire and to direction.

Get Off the Couch

 Many ancient cultures recognized the need for ensuring that there was a process for this sort of maturation as well as for the need to determine desires. In ancient Rome, one was not considered to be an adult until the age of 35 and at that time it was the beginning of allowing that person to run for office as well as to be a productive member of that society.

In short, many of these methods of the past are gone and there are many clients who end up on the couch looking for the answers to these fundamental questions like, who are they, and what do they want to do with their lives?

It is a question that is best asked in youth, rather than in later years when years are spent laboring in a profession that was not loved, or spent married to the wrong person.

A therapist can act as a coach, as much as a therapist, and to help you to identify the behaviors and goals which will propel you from the average into the extraordinary. These little questions that might have been asked in the past to an oracle are now making their way into the couch of the therapist.

How Can Education Change Things?

I'm not just talking about sitting in a university or classroom setting, but really taking the time to learn. Education is the great equalizer, it is the thing that can turn everything around in the life of a client and make a huge difference towards having a happy and a fulfilled life. When a client takes the time to invest in themselves and to work with a professional the result is instant. Instead of it being a situation where the therapist is pulling the client, it is a situation where the client is taking an active role in their long-term development.

Working towards the education of a client with a therapist is arming the client to ensure that there is an active undertaking that is a partnership towards the goals and the happiness of the client. When there has been a session to sit down and to map out the direction of the client, the next step is ensuring that there is a path for improvement as well as for real change for the client and for the therapist.

❖ What Are the Books Every Person Should Read?

There are several books out there that should be read by every person who desire to to educate themselves about their success, their lives, and their business. Education is one of the tools that will help a client to understand who they are and why they are in the position that they are in and for that reason it is very critical to ensure that there is a very viable reason for them to educate themselves both for their business and for their own growth.

❖ Here Are the Books that Everyone Should Read.

1. Think and Grow Rich: Napoleon Hill

This book has formed the basis for all the personal development books out there for the last 100 years. It has rewritten the rules on what should be expected out of a great book. This book is known to have created more millionaires than any other book that graced the shelves of a bookstore or library. It was the first of its kind and has sold over 60 million copies since its release. The book outlines the strategies of success that were practiced and outlined by all the titans of the industrial revolution. In addition to that, the book has proved to be one of the primary sources of inspiration and education for changing and transforming the lives of titans all over the world.

This book was commissioned by Carnegie and was then developed into a group of lectures and presentations which would seed the life of Napoleon Hill for the rest of his career and ensure that there was going to be a very clear and direct path to success for all the readers who came behind him.

2. The Work of Les Brown

When it comes to looking for a modern-day template, one of the best things to do is to look to the work of Les Brown. A titan in personal development he has worked to make sure he could work with Fortune 500 CEOs all over the country and has decided to help people who want real change to transform their companies as well as their mindsets. This is a great way to learn the habits which allow for an entrepreneur or a person who is looking for a roadmap to learn how to conquer his or her dreams.

3. The Work of Henry Ford

The work of Henry Ford is universal, as well as timeless. Ford had a vision of learning that encouraged others to listen to employees, as well as to leave the expertise to the experts. Instead of trying to specialize in everything. He hired those who were the smartest in their classification and could change the production world with his ideas.

The assembly line which was the beginning of modern manufacturing has changed and redefined the way that companies operated as well as thought about their business over the course of the last century.

4. Rockefeller Habits

If you are a business owner this is one of those books that you simply cannot ignore. It is one that will continue to pay its dividends and its returns time and time again with a very real set of habits that will ensure that it is possible for a business owner to be successful in any situation.

It was these secrets that Rockefeller put down in his books that have become many of the core teaching philosophies for many of the most successful companies in the world. For anyone who is wanting to successfully run a company and ensure the success of that company for years to come this is one of those tools that will prove an incredible purchase for years to come.

"Shoot for the moon and if you miss you will still be among the stars."-Les Brown

Chapter 4: What is the difference between coaching and therapy?

There are very few differences in coaching and therapy. Many people who work in both roles, which ensures they will meet the needs of any patient. By using the methods available in coaching and therapy, a successful outcome is more likely for the individual seeking help. Most coaches have worked with therapists in the past, providing them with adequate knowledge of the conscious mind, to employ the needed techniques for patients/clients.

There is limited time to establish a report, therefore, it's important to make sure there is a way to interact with the client in a manner that allows accommodations/growth that is necessary in the life of the patient. The couch will need to point out any major points needed to overcome in the initial meeting.

When it comes to key difference between the two, the main difference is the piece of paper. One thing important to note, is there may be many theories out there. Some relating to the model or practice of therapy. Many coaches out there, have a lot in common with the way that they can help people.

The goal when selecting a coach, is to determine if they are looking at someone's past, and the obstacles to peace for the client.

When you are working with someone whether they are on the phone, or there is a specific thing you are tracking you want to make sure that you can add real value and that means that you need to help them develop the tools necessary to alleviate suffering as well as know that you are going to make a real difference together.

When you are a therapist you are working with the experience as well as with the personality of the client which means that you need to make sure that you can help him or her understand all the emotions that they have that they may not be aware of. You want to make sure as well that you can be on the right track with the commitment that is made by the client to ensure that they are also on the same page with the process.

You want to know that you can adjust and to work with the client in a way that is going to help him or get to ensure that there are results that will be immediately helpful in the long term.

What is the Proper Behaviour for Interacting with a Coach or Therapist?

One thing that is a major issue in the long term for clients, coaches, and therapists is to understand what the role of proper protocol is for interacting and making sure that there is a clear role of communication as well to respond in the long term for all roles.

Whether you have a coach, or you have a therapist it is important to make sure that you are interacting with him or her in a way that is professional. It is very unprofessional to expect that there is going to be a response from all parties that is going to be instant on a regular basis. What that means is that if you are texting with your coach, this is not the way to ensure that you are going to be able to have access to the best and most professional relationship with them.

It doesn't mean that you can't communicate in this way, but what it does mean is that the expectation that they respond instantaneously might need be evaluated. Boundaries are important for the client as well as the coach or therapist. We want to ensure that this is a healthy relationship.

Why do Many Clients Fail at Coaching and at Therapy?

When it comes to making sure that you have clients who are going to be successful it is important to make sure that you can define a very clear set of rules and parameters that will have a way of allowing there to be a measure that there is success that is happening. What that means is that there needs to be a very specific procedure to have access to the accounting and the progress that is happening over the long term. Many of the coaches as well as the therapists fail to define a set of parameters which are going to assist with the process of allowing there to be a way to measure the success or the failure of the program.

It is important to make sure that there is a very specific way to measure the progress of the process. When there is a setback along the way there also needs to be a specific process to ensure that there is a way to measure the progress that is made and lost. That way in the beginning of the process when there is a setback it will ensure that there is going to be a swift correction.

What is the Missing Ingredient in the Sauce for Real and Meaningful Change?

When it comes to making sure that there is a real difference in the success or the failure of a method it is very important to look at the desire that has gone into the process. What that means is that there must be a real level of desire for change from the client. He or she must have reached the point that they are ready for real and meaningful change. When the commitment is real there will be a change and a difference in the way that things happen over the long term to making progress on the goal.

"Our deepest fear is not that we are inadequate. Our deepest fear is that we are powerful beyond measure. It is our light, not our darkness, that most frightens us. You're playing small does not serve the world. There is nothing enlightened about shrinking so that other people won't feel insecure around you. We are all meant to shine as children do. It's not just in some of us; it is in everyone. And as we let our own lights shine, we unconsciously give another people permission to do the same. As we are liberated from our own fear, our presence automatically liberates others." - Marianne Williamson

Chapter 5: Breakthrough Techniques

When it comes to the world of counseling, there has never been a more exciting time to be practicing, either as a coach or a therapist. Technology and the knowledge of the brain has changed everything that we knew about the way that the brain functioned and the way that things work.

The History of Psychology

When it comes to looking at psychology it is a relatively new science. Many people think of it as the study of behavior and mental process put together. There has always been an interest in the middle east and in Europe of the way that the mind works and understanding all the components of this process. Until the 1870's there was a fusion of psychology and philosophy. It was in the 1870's in Germany and in the United States that there was a clear change in the way that people looked at the brain and decided that it was time to learn more about the process. This came in 1879 when there was a laboratory that was dedicated to the study in 1879 in Germany.

This scientist was a man who was named Wilhelm Wundt and he was the first person to ever call himself a psychologist. In the USA, there were also many other scientists who were interested in the field a few of these included Herman Ebbinghaus who was a specialist in memory, William James who was a specialist in pragmatism, and finally Ivan Pavlov who was famous for his experiments in conditioning.

Get Off the Couch

There are many kinds of psychology that were brought to the USA by international doctors during the 1880's what that meant was that were many ways to ensure that these concepts became very common in western culture and became a part of everyday vernacular.

The History of Hypnotism

What people think of as hypnotism has been around forever. It was not until the 1880's however that there was an influx of hypnosis. What that meant was that by the early 20th century, it was a term that people were familiar with everywhere.

 One thing that was very disconnected for many people who were familiar with hypnotism was the way that it worked and how it was possible to have access to all the different quadrants of the mind.

There were also many other traditions that go all the way back to the ancient Greeks that were in fact very similar to hypnotism and that was called Temple Sleeping. When there was an ailment that was not solvable through ancient medicine the Greeks believed that the way to solve this was to allow the person with the ailment to sleep in the temple of the god of health.

There when the patient was in the temple, he or she would have inspired dreams which would lead to a placebo effect. One thing that is not clear from modern archaeology was if this was an opium induced state or if it was one that was derived from hypnotism. There are many studies out there seeking to get to the bottom of this currently.

Get Off the Couch

When it comes to the history of modern hypnosis it is something that needs to be looked at with detail as it is something that was clear that it was always useful but also something that was not completely understood.

When it comes to the origins of the modern practice it comes from Frans Mesmer who was practicing from 1737-1815. He used a method that was known as mesmerism, which is a popular term for being fixated on something even today. He could prove the powers of the medium and to ensure that it was possible to help people who had disorders. He had a very famous case when he was working with a pianist who was named Paradis, she had a fit of hysteria that caused blindness.

This indicated that she was going to not be able to perform her job with the blindness. Mesmer decided that the thing to do was to make sure that she was able to learn the ways to follow movements and to be in a trancelike state to learn long hand movements. She was then able to have a moment in her blindness where she could then see color and handle daylight.

 She reverted to her previous condition however when she was returned to her family and there were many accusations that took place at that point against Mesmer.

Many of his theories were then explored by other pioneers in the field such as John Elliot son and James Esdaile who were both British surgeons. Both men used the techniques of the trancelike state to perform amputations and to ensure that it was possible to put people under so that they were not going to feel any pain while they were being operated on.

Get Off the Couch

James Braid was called and considered the father of hypnosis. He was active from 1795-1860 and is thought to have approached the issue and the topic from a very scientific perspective which made his interest very tactical and easier for others to accept. When looking at the topic in the past there were many who considered it almost to be occult more than anything else. When it came to Braid he also coined the term hypnosis itself.

Braid was a doctor and was always fascinated by the way that people could pay attention to different aspects of a candle flame that was flickering in his office. One thing that was very interesting to the doctor was the state of mind that he could observe in the patients when they were focusing on the flame.

What this meant for Braid was that it was important to make sure that there were other demonstrations and experiments that took place such as seeing the level of fixation as well as the level of attention that was paid by the patient. There were many cases that he looked at that meant that it was possible to for people to be cured from headaches as well as skin conditions with hypnosis.

In the 20th century there were many others who could really add to the academic study of hypnosis. This came from Pierre Janet, Clark Hull, and Sigmund Freud. Freud used hypnosis in his early practices. Another very interesting researcher is that of Emile Coue who was a practitioner of auto suggestion and then decided to also consider self-hypnosis.

He saw that it was possible to see the way that the imagination could be used to solve problems if the client was involved. What this also means is that it was possible as well to make sure that it was something that could be done with clients to teach them how to focus on the process.

There were two other major figures that really made a very large difference in the process, these doctors were Milton H. Erickson and Dave Elman. When it came to the work of Erickson, he was focusing on what is referred to as indirect hypnosis. Which was based on the language patterns that were a part of the perceptions of people's thoughts of themselves. What that meant was that it was possible to make sure that it was achieved using inductions and using language that would be helpful to the long-term hypnosis of the patient. In addition to that, it was possible to make sure that hypnosis would be very helpful for a person if it was meaningful. That meant that the doctor needed to make sure that he could understand the learnings and the process of the patient.

Elman is not as well-known, but he wrote a book that was a textbook for many. Elman could look at the way that stage hypnotism and therapy were used for therapy. He utilized this to achieve results almost instantly.

These techniques are used in the current practice of therapy. This ensures there will be an instant solution, which comes with techniques that are guided by the patient.

What is NLP?

NLP stands for Neuro Linguistic Programing and it is a composite of the three most important parts of human experience: those are neurology, language, and programming. It is the nerve system that will determine how people respond and communicate with one another and the way that people create models of the world. What that means is that there is a deep level of programming that dictates the way that information is processed and the way that behavior is handled.

The link between the systems exists between the mind, the body and the behavior of the subject.

When it comes to the schools of thought that are surrounding NLP it is related to the entire experience of being a person. The process is a 3D experience that allows for competence as well as flexibility in the way that people respond the thinking and to processes. What that means is that there are many tools out there that are a part of the process that will allow for there to be many other states of excellence. What that means is that there is a system of beliefs that are out there for every level of people and there are ideas as well about what humanity encompasses. When looking as well at NLP it is also a process of self-discovery for the person who is on a mission. There is a part of the process that is also related to the aspects of the spiritual human experience. NLP is a new system of vision and possibility for the entire experience.

Richard Bandler: The Father of NLP

When it comes to NLP, there is no one who is more influential than the father and founder of the process Richard Bandler. He is a trainer as well as an author who was interested in seeing how it was possible to bend the boundaries of reality and ensure that people could use a blend of techniques and patterns of Hypnotism and NLP. There are other systems that were designed by the master such as Design Human Engineering and Neuro Hypnotic Repatterning.

The work of Bandler has changed the way that people think about hypnosis as well as the way that they interact with the subject matter. Bandler was a big part of the edit of the book that was called The Gestalt Approach, this was a book that spoke about how therapy worked and how it was possible to have access to the best options out there using hypnosis.

What is So Different About NLP?

NLP ensures that it can look at and explore the connection that exists between the process and language. What that means is that it is possible for people to model the skills of exceptional talent and allow patients to have access to treatments that otherwise would be difficult to have.

If there is an issue that a patient has been having, through the implementation of NLP it is possible to make sure that all the issues that have been held by the patient in the past can be treated almost instantly. These are things like the cold, allergies, and other issues like substance abuse.

Get Off the Couch

The Subjectivity of the World

Bandler could realize and to capitalize on the fact that the world is in fact a very subjective experience. What that means is that there are many ways which the world is experienced and most of them are done by the 5 senses. What that also means is that it is possible to take the regular senses and then rehearse an activity in the mind so that it is possible to visualize the experience and ensure that there is a way to experience and prepare for the outcome of the situation. This means is there are many ways as well that the behaviors that we use every day can be looked at as subjective representations.

The behavior can have many sense based representations that mean that it is possible to have a mix of verbal as well as nonverbal communication for those that are not the best at being able to use only visual stimuli. NLP also looks at the way that it is possible to blend consciousness and subconsciousness and that means that it is possible to see that the awareness of a person is directly connected to the part of the mind that is being used at that moment.

NLP utilizes modeling, which means that it is possible to reproduce the excellence of any trait in any activity with the representations that need to be had in the moment for the person who is working with the condition. That means that the work that is done by the therapist can be done quickly and ambitiously with the right amount of influence.

There are many ways to understand NLP. One of those ways is to look at how it is possible to look at the mindset of the patient and to see how the information and the goals can be merged for the better processing. This is done using the responses of the client as well as the pacing and the interaction of the verbal and the nonverbal information.

This means it is important for the doctor to see how the verbal as well as the nonverbal communication of the patient is handled, and these techniques must be put together to ensure that there is a pattern for interaction as well as for the way that real progress can be made.

When it comes to making sure that the methods are successful, a large part of that is allowing for there to be a very clear relationship that happens with the practitioner as well as with the client. What that means is that there needs to be a merge of nonverbal and verbal communication from both sides so that it is possible for the professional relationships and the personal ones to merge and allow for there to be the perfect fusion of method and response to stimuli.

How Are These Techniques Used for Real Change?

When it comes to creating real change, there are many things about NLP and hypnotism that when used together can change the realities of the patient once and for all. One thing that is important to understand is the fusion of the use of the conscious and subconscious mind. Whether or not the person who wants the change realizes it or not the conscious mind is only scratching the surface of the information that is contained by the subconscious mind. This is the same reason that there are so many failures when there are traditional means of therapy.

Get Off the Couch

There is no way that it is possible for those who are undergoing the technique to really break beyond their own programming and it takes a toll on those who are looking to find a solution through traditional means of therapy. There are often setbacks and that means that the patient can get very frustrated.

When it comes to the work that must be done, using traditional techniques can be very hard for many of the patients because they are already in a place where they need more structure. What that also means is that it is not possible to have access to the best choices when they are looking for an instant solution. Utilizing the methods of NLP and hypnotism it is possible for the client to see instant results if the client places trust in the method and in the doctor.

Change According to the Doctor

One thing that is very important to the entire practice of NLP is understanding that it is not just about the mind it is also about the body. Whatever the condition is that is being treated by the doctor, it is something that is a part of both the mind and the body.

For these reasons, it is very important for the client to understand that to have real meaningful change there must be a change in the mind and the body to ensure that there is an upgrade in health. Many of the practitioners of NLP are also into organic diets and other methods of calming the body and mind and assisting with the fusion of the two.

Get Off the Couch

The Work of Dr. Maritsa Yzaguirre-Kelley

Dr. Yzaguirre-Kelley is a yoga instructor as well as a vegan. She focuses on teaching her clients to live a life that is a balance between a sound mind and a sound body. Her methods are revolutionary as she blends the techniques of NLP, hypnotism, and other alternative methods, so at the end of the day she places complete confidence and power of the client back into their hands. One of the main ideas that she teaches her clients, is that they are in fact whole. Many other doctors or therapist will label a client as having something wrong - but let's face it…. a diagnosis is a label that sticks with a person forever and sometimes can have negative consequences for the patient.

Dr. Yzaguirre-Kelley focuses on reminding the patient that all the power to change as well as the method to do it is already in the client. The mechanism for real and groundbreaking change can be brought about by taking the client and helping them to get unstuck. Patients find themselves getting stuck quite frequently in ways that are very hard to change.

When there is a pattern in which a client gets stuck, it takes a practitioner using modeling, and deleting the imprinting that happened to a person to give them the response to the stimuli that they have in that situation.

Whether the client knows it or not in every moment all people are constantly being affected by their environment and the things around them. What that means for the client is that if they came from a toxic environment and a bad situation, there is going to be a simple repeat of this situation until the pattern is broken. These patterns are mental as much as they are physical and that means that it is important to make sure that it is possible to break them in a way that will help the client to get beyond their stuck position.

The fusion of these techniques as well as the empowerment and the tools to give the client real change ensure that he or she will be able to have a new life with a new situation through the right guidance.

Dr. Yzaguirre-Kelley seeks a whole solution for her clients and can make real change that happens fast for the client. She reminds the client that he or she already has all the tools that are necessary to make real change inside of them. It is merely opening themselves to the change and allowing the foundations of the house to be rebuilt with a trusted architect at their side.

"Change is messy in the beginning, hard in the middle, and beautiful at the end." - Robin Sharma

Chapter 6: How to Get Your Clients off The Couch

If you are a doctor or therapist, one of the most important things that you need to realize is that you are doing no one any good by keeping them on the couch. You are enabling that client to feel subpar, to feel broken, as if there is something that is wrong with him or her. This also in some ways makes you an unethical practitioner.

What is the entire purpose of therapy after all any kind? The entire goal is to put the power of the situation and the client back into their own hands and to ensure that they can have a happy life.

When someone comes to you with a problem the entire process is to help them and to make sure that you are getting to the root of the problem. Many do not do this in the right sense because they do not focus on the client and they do not focus on their needs.

 They instead allow the client to come and be on their couch for many years and to pour more and more money into sessions that at the end of the day are not helping the client with the main issue because of possibly having no clear-cut direction to the goals and objectives that needed to be met.

What Will Facilitate Permanent Change?

When it comes to the way that therapist run their businesses there are many out there who are focused on continuing to bring the revenue in but are not focusing on getting their clients off the couch. What that means is that there is a lack of focus from the therapist on how they can run their businesses in a way that will ensure that they are profitable.

This is one of the most important things to make real change in the business and one of the ways that they make a profit. As a therapist, it is important to realize that you are also a small business owner. What that means is that you must take responsibility for the fiscal health of the company.

What this means is that you want to make sure that you are doing the best possible things for your business. What that means is that you need to make sure that you have access to the best methods for your company and that as a business owner you need to master all the Rockefeller Habits. This is a sure-fire way to make sure that you are going to be successful.

At the beginning of the century there were many titans who were making their way in every industry and that meant that there was a need for a blueprint that would ensure that there would be success for upcoming ventures and in different industries.

Rockefeller knew that the way to dominate every industry was to make sure that it was possible to have a plan that would work out of the box each time and ensure that there was going to be a way to present a business model that would work for everyone. The Rockefeller method has been applied to practices all over the world and guarantees an incredible result when it is implemented.

Get Off the Couch

There are many consulting firms that have taken the method and have become passionate about implementing it all over the world with the process of transformation and change. You will see that there are 5 fundamental and unshakeable tenants of the model.

❖ Nail your Priorities!

You want to make sure that you have around 5 priorities for a year, that means that you are going to have one that you can do per quarter which will ensure that you are always on top of your strategy and that you are ready to go. You want to know that you are really making progress and that you can focus on something that is going to be digestible and that will ensure that all the milestones are consumable to the entire team.

❖ Have a Communication Pattern

Let's face it, everything has a rhythm and that means that your communications need to as well.

It is very important for your employees to know what to expect and how they should be able to communicate with a quick look at an email or with a quick update from you. When reading the book and learning the method, you want to make sure that you are creating something that is going to be meaningful and something that is going to help you to be able to hit all your targets.

In addition to that, it is important to think about how you are going to be able to have access to move forward on all your other goals daily. You want to make sure that you have a very early and punctual meeting that gets all members to dedicate themselves to the process as well as to the mission that is being laid out.

If you have team members who are late, you will know the lack of dedication that they have to the mission of the company. In addition to that, you will also want to make sure that you take the time to have the remote members of the team be available to know that they are also a part of the group.

Annual summits are a great way to include everyone and to ensure that it is possible to have access to all the best choices for the team in partnership and in excellence.

❖ Use the Data!

It is very important to realize and to remember that there are many ways to focus on the success of a company and part of it is to allow the numbers to speak for themselves. They outline very clearly what works and what does not work. What this means is that as a business owner regardless of how something may feel personally it is critical to make sure that you are willing to make the decisions for business that need to be made.

That will enable you as well to ensure that you are always going to know that you are going to be making the best choices to meet your bottom line. Sometimes the efficient and the humanitarian decisions do not align but you have a business to run.

❖ Finding the Wild Card!

You must know what the wild card is and make sure that you are going to be able to find the way to respond to the things that hit you and to the things that are important. What that means is that as a business owner you need to know what the place is that your company needs help in and find ways to overcome that weakness. That means that on a regular basis you need to be doing all you can to analyze and determine where your failures and where your weaknesses are so that you are going to be able to overcome them with flying colors.

❖ Prepare for Anything!

One thing that you need to make sure that you are doing is planning. That means that you need to have a different plan for every phase of your life. You will want to make sure that you have a plan for each year as well as for 10 years moving forward.

While that may sound a bit excessive, it is important to make sure that you have a very clear path to success and you want to sure that you are going to know that you have measurable milestones.

❖ What Are the Key Takeaways?

As a business owner, you need to make sure that you have really looked at your practice and have made sure that you are looking that will allow you to make sure that you are going to create real transformation and change.

❖ What Happens When You Master These Practices?

When it comes to the practices that are out there, there are few people who have been more successful than the Rockefellers. They have created a perfect method that will ensure that it is possible to offer a real plan of transformation and change that will allow you to have a secret sauce against your competition. There are tons of books out there, but there are few that are tried and tested in the same way that Mastering the Rockefeller Methods are.

❖ How Can You Change Everything in 15 Minutes?

When you decide that you are going to make real change, you need to understand that as a business owner or as a client, the commitment and the change must come from you. As I always tell my clients, "the magic is within you and always has been."

When someone gives you the idea that you are broken and that you cannot change, whether they know it or not they are making sure that you are not going to be able to affect real change. That is crippling to you and allows you to not feel that you are going to be able to make change. It is the time to stop thinking that the therapist is ever classifying you as having an issue. What that means is that you can change whatever you want whenever you want.

Using NLP and Hypnotism for Real Change

When it comes to NLP and Hypnotism they are both very real things and they work differently. There are many different processes as well as trials that will allow you to be able to see the evidence of NLP and Hypnotism. There are many institutions out there as well that will ensure that you are able to see the different classifications.

NLP is the fusion of the conscious and the subconscious mind through the practice of a coach who can guide the patient to the results that he or she is seeking. As a doctor, the relationship and the way that words are used allows for there to be a connection to the patient and to the doctor. The experiences of NLP are visual, gustatory, auditory, tactile, and olfactory and it is the job of the coach to take the patient through the experience that they are trying to model to ensure that he or she can have the experience that will help them to overcome the matter that they are dealing with at that moment.

One thing that is different about NLP and hypnotism is that there is active participation from the patient in the experience and that means that he or she needs to have the confidence in the doctor to ensure that there is going to be a positive result. When there is no the participation from the patient, there are many things that can happen and yet there is no sort of participation from the patient it is all left in the hands of the doctor. The process that happens with hypnotism is completely subconscious and that means that it will continue to be something that the doctor is driving, it is a completely passive experience.

The military has used hypnotism for many years to ensure that it was possible to have the best outcome when dealing with soldiers. There have been many experiments in the role of hypnotism which have allowed for there to be a complete understanding of the mind and the way that people are able to compartmentalize situations as well as to know how they are going to deal with situations that may happen in the future.

Get Off the Couch

Hypnotism has become one of the most fundamental parts of being able to process an experience or an issue that has happened to a soldier during battle.

One way that hypnotism has taken center stage is using magic. There are many illusionists out there who have figured out how to use NLP and hypnotism in their shows to delight the audience and to show the power of the techniques. One of the most famous magicians out there who has done this is Darren Brown.

The Magic of the Mind with Darren Brown

Darren Brown is one of those illusionists who knows how to use the power of the mind on stage and who has actively impressed the audiences around the world with his technique. Brown uses a mix of suggestion, psychology, magic, and shows how to control other people as well. There are many critics out there who have sought to make sure that they are able to focus as well on the process of trying to debunk him. One thing that is very clear is that there are many ways to look at hypnotism as well as at other kinds of techniques that have been used on the stage.

There are many critics who have sought to see how it is possible to be able to have such access to fooling the minds of the populace, but few have been able to respond over the long term. What that means is that the fusion of the techniques is something that has become an artform.

Brown is a very talented performer who knows how it is possible to work with the audience in a way that it is possible to combine many factors for success. He uses magic and hypnosis in some real and amazing ways. One of the most important things is that it is necessary to know how to distinguish between magic and spells.

This means that it is possible to know what is happening. No one seems to know for sure what happens when hypnosis works but there has been a change in the way that people interact and in the way that they are able to communicate with each other. What that means is that it is important to see the way that the interaction happens and realize that it is close to waking consciousness.

What that also means is that it is helpful to consider the eyes of the spectator when they are told to sleep and see the way that they response. You will see that there are many people who do not know what they are going to do, and they also do not know how they are going to handle the situation.

You will see that there are many people sometimes and it appears when they are watching almost as if from the perspective of a third person who is on stage. There are many ways that it is possible for Brown to use his gifts of hypnosis through suggestion in a way that will make sure that there is going to be a successful hypnotic process.

There are many other illusionists who have utilized the power of hypnosis and other methods for many years such as crises Angel and Harry Houdini. Brown is now taking this discussion to a whole new level by interacting with others who have created a habit into wanting to know how it works and how it is possible to have large groups of people who go through the same experience over and over.

New Discoveries About Harry Houdini

One thing that has stunned many people as of late is the idea that Harry Houdini used hypnosis in his shows. From his beginning, iconic experience at the Orpheum in which he held the stage for 23 days and delighted the audience, to his credit he was performing things that had never been seen by the audience and that means that it was in fact his way of interacting with the crowd and his showmanship which ensured that there was a state of hypnosis that was going to pass over all those who were watching his presentation.

The work of Houdini is so good that it means there are many ways that it is possible to see it in play both from the perspective of seeing the way that the crowd reacted to it and the way that the artist used it himself to ensure that he could overcome any situation that he might face.

When it comes to being able to master the body and knowing that he was going to be do the show and know that his body was going to be able to handle the limits that it had been pushed to.

Part of what it means is that there is no limit to the way that the brain can be used to process information and to the way that these tools can be used.

Criss Angel as one of the most successful magicians in the world has confessed to using hypnosis as well as programming to ensure that he is able to surpass his own boundaries on a regular basis and ensure that he is always using the best options out there for his audience to see a show of epic proportions.

NLP and hypnosis when they are put together are a way to ensure that there is always going to be a huge strength on the side of the body to ensure and allow him to create the same works that Houdini did while adding his own elements to surpass him.

There has been recent study done on Houdini and there are countless news articles that reference the way that he has learned how to hypnotize the audience and has trained the body on how it should be able to endure anything.

The potential for NLP as well as for the way that the process is carried out ensures that it is possible to unlock the potential of any level of excellence and for that situation to be modeled to the patient with the assistance of the right doctor.

"Perfection is not attainable but if we try hard enough excellence is." - Vince Lombardi

Afterthought NLP Unlocking the Value

When it comes to NLP one thing that many people forget is that we are spiritual beings that are having a human experience. One thing that has also been very helpful for many patients is considering regressive therapy. When there is an issue that seems to rear its head in the lives of patients repeatedly, it is something that must be corrected whether it is from a past or a current situation. The result of all of that is the same and it means that there is a need to ensure that in the future the situation does not raise its ugly head.

There are many professionals out there like Dr. Brian Weiss who are specialists who use NLP and hypnotism to make sure that they can assist with past life anxieties and issues. This happened to the doctor when he had a patient who was being hypnotized and was recounting the issues she had and then was also getting messages from the spaces that existed between lives.

One thing that became the mission of Dr. Weiss was to take his education to the bleeding edge of the world with his practices and with his techniques.

In addition to this, he has also trained many other doctors all over the world in how to open the lives of their patients by looking at past life memories. When looking at the YouTube channel of Dr. Weiss it is immediately clear to the viewer why he is a bestselling author and why he has also won many Emmys. His bestselling book called Many Lives Many Masters has explained to patients all over the world how it is possible for there to be places where people get stuck whether intentionally or unintentionally and that means that it is the job of a good doctor to help the client to find the next step and to ensure that the issues are dealt with.

The Power of NLP and Hypnosis

The power of these tools is beginning to be understood in a way that will transform the current beliefs of what is possible.

Get Off the Couch

As a patient who may have gotten stuck along the path to greatness, you owe it to yourself to make sure that you're ready for the challenges that this life throws at you and to make sure that you have found the path to happiness and fulfillment. This is your opportunity to make sure that you are going to take things to the next level as well as to ensure that you have access to the best options out there. In the information age, there is no reason for all of us not to harness our greatness and to take things to the next level. All the tools you have ever needed and all the strength you have wanted are within you. It is your time to shine.

"You are the key to your solution and to your destiny. You have the power." - Dr. Maritsa Yzaguirre-Kelley

Chapter 7: Services of Dr. Yzaguirre-Kelley

Are you ready? Change doesn't always wait sometimes it's sudden. We must however be confident in the knowledge that this too will bring me nothing but good. Check out and learn about some of the services we provide.

Alternative Therapies and Retreats

There are so many different modalities when it comes to counseling. It's not a one size fits all. I like to make sure my clients get what they need. Some therapy tools I utilize with my clients are cognitive behavioral therapy, solution focused therapy, behavior therapy, and holistic/integrative therapy. The holistic/integrative approach may include bioenergetics, reiki, breath work, yoga, hypnosis, and nutritional guidance.

Counselling Solutions

What is counseling? Who benefits from counseling? What can I expect? Counseling is a process of self-discovery that can help people learn how to deal more effectively with situations in their lives such as depression, addiction and substance abuse, stress, problems with self-esteem, grief, issues related to mental and emotional health, and relational problems. This process helps people feel more comfortable with themselves, others, and helps develop some of the skills needed to deal with the tensions that come from inside.

Get Off the Couch

The therapy/counseling process helps people get "unstuck".
Through the development of insight and increased self-
awareness, people can gain a better understanding of their
own behavior and the issues, feelings and events that
motivate them. The most useful benefit of therapy is often an
improvement in health and wellbeing. This often translates into
increased self-confidence, productivity and a greater sense of
vitality and peace of mind. People of any age can grow and
profit from the experience of therapy.

There is no "wrong" time to begin! Counseling is a type of
learning about oneself.

- ✓ Relationships issues

- ✓ Family issues

- ✓ Self-esteem issues

- ✓ Depression

- ✓ Anxiety/stress

- ✓ Anger Management

- ✓ Substance Abuse Evaluations

Health and Holistic Practices

Your food choices each day affect your health — how you feel
today, tomorrow, and in the future.

Get Off the Couch

Good nutrition is an important part of leading a healthy lifestyle. Combined with physical activity, your diet can help you to reach and maintain a healthy weight, reduce your risk of chronic diseases (like heart disease and cancer), and promote your overall health.

The Impact of Nutrition on Your Health

The link between good nutrition and healthy weight, reduced chronic disease risk, and overall health is too important to ignore. By taking steps to eat healthy, you'll be on your way to getting the nutrients your body needs to stay healthy, active, and strong. As with physical activity, making small changes in your diet can go a long way, and it's easier than you think!

Check out "IT WORKS" to get you on track and keep you there!

Substance Abuse and Health Issues

Evaluations are recommended for a variety of reasons. Evaluations could be the result of a court order from a recent arrest (dui, possession, or public intoxication), work ordered, or due to custody/divorce recommendations.

Regardless of the reason for the evaluation it is important to have a therapist who is highly experienced in these evaluations as well as the documentation that is needed for the parties requesting the evaluation.

I worked as the forensic liaison for Palm Beach County courts working with both county, state, and federal mental health and substance related cases. I have more than 10 years working and owning Substance Abuse and Mental Health Treatment facilities. I was responsible for administering evaluations, as well as, training staff on proper clinical documentation as a qualified supervisor and training specialist.

About the Author

My name is Maritsa Yzaguirre-Kelley. I started out with a Masters in Mental Health Counseling and I went to work for one of the largest drug and alcohol treatment centers in the country as their Executive director. I hold certificates in Alternative Medicine, Clinical Hypnosis, and NLP. I went on to complete my doctorate in counseling as well.

My motivation for starting my coaching/consultation company, was so I can help professionals whose work has over taken their lives, break free and live.

I focus on teaching clients to live a life that is a balance between a sound mind and a sound body. My methods are revolutionary, as I blend the techniques of NLP, hypnotism, and other alternative methods, such as yoga.

I call South Florida my home even though I was born in Massachusetts. I have 2 boys, 3 dogs, and of course my amazing husband. We enjoy playing golf, going to the beach, gym, and playing with the kids. If I was still working in corporate being able to have that quality time to do the things I enjoy with the people I love would be unheard of.

For more information Visit:

http://www.maximizewithrits.com
Or Email: Rits@Maximizewithrits.com
Phone Number: 561-288-6548

www.ingramcontent.com/pod-product-compliance
Lightning Source LLC
Chambersburg PA
CBHW031423250726
48656CB00002B/809